NORTH DEVON

-•- *The Golden Years* -•-

COMPILED BY PETER CHRISTIE

HALSGROVE

First published in Great Britain in 2002

For Nettie

British Library Cataloguing-in-Publication Data
A CIP record for this title is available from the British Library

ISBN 1 84114 180 1

HALSGROVE

Halsgrove House
Lower Moor Way
Tiverton, Devon EX16 6SS
Tel: 01884 243242
Fax: 01884 243325
email: sales@halsgrove.com
website: www.halsgrove.com

Printed and bound by
Bookcraft Ltd., Midsomer Norton

Whilst every care has been taken to ensure the accuracy of the information contained in this book, the author disclaims responsibility for any mistakes which may have inadvertently been included.

FOREWORD

Henry Ford had it wrong when he declared that history was 'bunk'. History shapes us and roots us; paints pictures for us of our role in the grand scheme of things. That is why history fascinates us. That is never more so, in my experience, than with history we can almost touch. Whenever the *North Devon Journal* publishes a photograph taken within living memory, the response is always phenomenal, sparking as it does recollections of old names, faces and places.

Which is why it is such a joy to see that Peter Christie's latest look at the history of North Devon concentrates on the more recent past of the region. We have seen many of the more 'sepia tinted' collections of old photographs which feature this area, but few which span the 1940s to '60s. Contained within these pages is a fascinating collection of the region's past from not so long ago. Some locations and ways of life have changed forever, but others remain refreshingly familiar. The fact that many of the images are taken from the files of the *Journal* (or *Journal-Herald* as it was in those days) is also very welcome, showing off, as it does, an element of the wonderful archive we have amassed over the years.

I am sure a number of the pictures will spark a memory or two among many of you. I hope you enjoy reading it as much as I have.

Andy Cooper
Managing Editor, *North Devon Journal*
May 2002

Local children have played on the quay at Appledore for generations and this photograph from April 1953 shows a group of youngsters playing at 'shop', using a seat as their shop counter.

INTRODUCTION

As someone who usually writes about 'real' history, i.e. happenings in the nineteenth century or earlier, it came as a surprise to be asked to work on a book set in the late 1940s and '50s. I was born in 1950 and it is an odd feeling to realise you are now history. It was even more unsettling, however, to start the book and realise just how much the world has changed in the last 50 years – often, it seems, without us really noticing.

This very quickly became apparent when I began sorting through a collection of some 5,000 glass negatives from these decades. Originally taken by photographers working for the *North Devon Journal* (then called the *North Devon Journal-Herald*), the plates had been due to be thrown out until providentially being given to the North Devon Athenaeum many years ago. Here they have lain unconsulted and unused ever since. A quick perusal of just a few boxes revealed the riches they contained. Over several months I examined every plate and managed, with some difficulty, to choose the 300 or so you now see before you. Although some had been printed in the newspaper, most had not and therefore appear here in public for the first time.

Many were undated and some carried no indication of what they were, so identifying them and writing captions has not been straightforward. In searching out the material, however, I have discovered a lot of things I never knew, so it has been an enjoyable learning experience. In most cases I have left the photographs to speak for themselves, the captions give a date, place and a brief description of the event pictured for the most part. But look at the details, often in the background, which in many cases are just as fascinating as the main subject matter. Especially intriguing are the clothes, the advertising posters and the décor in interior views.

Any errors (and I am certain there are some) are mine alone. I say this because I would not have been able to compile the book without the invaluable help of the North Devon Athenaeum staff, Les Franklin and Marjorie Snetzler, and the Local Studies Librarian Deborah Gahan, whom I thank profusely. Thanks are also due to my fellow directors of the North Devon Athenaeum who have allowed me access to the collection and to Naomi Cudmore of Halsgrove, who has acted as midwife to the volume.

I would have liked to have used many more photographs but space was limited – so if this book is successful perhaps I will produce another – and could I request that if you have any photographs from the period 1940–65 and would like to see them in print please contact me via the Athenaeum in Tuly Street, Barnstaple. North Devon is a very special area and people have been photographing it for over 150 years now so there must be a wealth of images out there.

I hope you enjoy the book and it brings back memories for those old enough to recall the period, and gives you an idea of life from 50 years ago if you are too young to remember.

Peter Christie

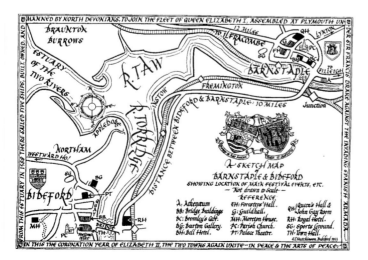

Map drawn for the Taw and Torridge Festival of 1953 by Sheila Hutchinson.

❧ CONTENTS ☙

CHAPTER ONE
THE *NORTH DEVON JOURNAL-HERALD*

Most of the photographs in this volume were taken for the *North Devon Journal-Herald* newspaper. Founded in July 1824 as the *North Devon Journal*, the paper joined with the *North Devon Herald* in March 1941. During the years covered by this book there were two editors.

In this photo we see Hugh McWhinnie, who had been editor of the *Herald* and became deputy editor of the new paper, rising to be editor over the years 1947–50. He was famous as a stickler for perfection, it being noted that: 'He would halt the press to correct a comma found out of place.'

He was succeeded by Bob Bale. The son of a local journalist, he attended West Buckland School and began work with the *Western Morning News* in 1939. After war service in the Royal Artillery he rejoined his old paper and then moved to the *North Devon Journal-Herald*, becoming editor in 1949 – a post he held until 1982. Under his control the paper doubled its circulation from 14,800 to 29,000.

In January 1954 the *Journal-Herald* incorporated the *Ilfracombe Chronicle*. It had been taken over by the *Journal-Herald* some years before but kept its separate identity, as is evident from this photograph of the office in Northfield Road in 1951. At the time of the takeover, the new enlarged paper noted that 'The new publication will give the whole of North Devon, and particularly Ilfracombe, an even higher standard of news service, unrivalled advertising facilities and more pages for THE SAME PRICE – THREEPENCE.'

The *Journal-Herald* was renowned as a good employer and many of its employees worked for the company for years. Joe Holwill of Stoke Rivers was one, and here, in October 1956, he beams on his retirement day after an incredible 56 years as a typesetter on the paper.

This series of photographs shows the rebuilding of the *Journal-Herald* offices in High Street, Barnstaple. Originally used to produce the paper in 1853, the need for change became pressing and in 1956 the staff moved to 11 Joy Street, whilst the old building was gutted and completely rebuilt. A 14-strong work team from Messrs Spencer Ltd of Plymouth removed 600 tons of rubble and replaced it with 100,000 bricks, 300 tons of concrete, 100 tons of steel and large amounts of woodwork – the latter from the Barnstaple firm of Shapland & Petter. The new building was brought into use in July 1957 and as well as housing the *Journal-Herald* also provided premises for the *Western Morning News* and the *Express & Echo.*

The original building prior to work starting.

This is a good example of how details in these photographs are often just as interesting as the main focus. In the above picture of the building site showing the erection of the steel girder skeleton an anachronistic looking horse-drawn milk cart was captured during deliveries. The cart belonged to Watt's Dairy which had been established in 1896 in premises in Boutport Street. Though not visible here, an echo of the 1950s is seen in the inscription on the cart's side 'Producer of Tuberculin Tested Milk'.

The hotch-potch of old buildings at the rear of the premises are removed and replaced.

Nearing completion.

The frontage as we know it in 2002 is virtually finished.

Whilst the building work went on the staff continued with their work, albeit in fairly spartan conditions as the top two photographs show. That the wait was worth it is clear from the final view (left) which shows the new office up and running.

CHAPTER TWO
❧ SETTLEMENTS ❧

One of the most severe problems facing young couples in Britain in the post-war years was the shortage of houses owing to war damage, the 'baby boom' and slum clearance programmes. This shortage explains this photograph of a house in Castle Street, Combe Martin built over just five weeks in January–February 1952. The builder, A.H. Norman, had been given his government licence to build the house on 1 January and by dint of hard effort managed to complete its construction in so short a period of time.

A little earlier, Bideford Borough Council decided to meet its housing shortage by constructing 'prefabs'. The first of the 50 planned prefabricated houses was opened on the Grenville Estate in April 1946. The opening ceremony was carried out by the Mayor, Councillor W.H. Chubb. The estate still exists but long ago brick-built houses replaced the utilitarian but much loved prefabs.

As each settlement saw its first council houses built the occasion was recorded for posterity. The first photograph shows new houses in Dolton around 1949 with proud tenants standing outside.

In South Molton the local authority developed new council housing in South Street and here we see operations in full flow in December 1951. It was noted that work had started on 2 October and 'according to the surveyor the first house should be ready for occupation by Easter.' As we have seen, such speed was not uncommon.

After the Second World War Barnstaple Council took a long, hard look at the state of houses in the borough and decided on wholesale demolition. Among the 700 substandard properties cleared away were many in the Derby area of the town including Vicarage Street, seen here just before operations began in December 1956.

The photograph on the right shows the Barnstaple Mayor, Dr King, and Alderman, Walter Thomas, using a mechanical shovel to start the ten-year clearance scheme in Corser Street.

Before clearance began the Barnstaple Sanitary Inspector, W. Rodgers, visited all the chosen properties and certified them as 'unfit for human habitation' – a decision opposed by just ten owners, which gives some idea of how bad they must have been.

Garden Court was typical of the small lanes and rows of houses that were demolished. Originally called Myrtle Place, this court was behind today's present Post Office at the corner of Queen Street and Boutport Street. The gates at the back lead to a disused Nonconformist burial-ground and were locally called 'Ghouls Gates'.

A view of Corser Street in the Derby district of Barnstaple. First laid out in 1827 and named Boden's Row after its builder (and local lace factory owner), John Boden, it had its name changed when Boden's daughter married Revd John Corser. Traditionally this area of Barnstaple was where policemen only went in pairs and it certainly has a 'colourful' history, but is still remembered today for its strong community spirit. The street was amongst the first demolished in the great clearance.

Another of the old areas to go was Pengelly's Court. This very narrow and overcrowded collection of houses was behind today's 'Halifax' building and was actually accessed by an entry from the High Street. Remnants of it are still to be found behind the cinema in Boutport Street.

A market cart outside the Barnstaple Pannier Market in Butcher's Row. Although not obvious from this photograph, traffic jams of horse-drawn carts were just as common as those of cars today in the narrow streets around the market, and in their own way were just as polluting as modern forms of transport!

Ilfracombe pier is a well-loved attraction in the resort town. It was possibly first constructed 700 years ago and was enlarged in both 1829 and 1874. During the Second World War, however, it was partly demolished as a precautionary measure against Nazi invaders landing there. Following hostilities it was declared unsafe.

Eventually the local council decided to rebuild the structure and these photographs from April 1950 onwards show the reconstruction of the south landing well under way.

The arrival of electricity in many small communities in North Devon meant that for the first time street lighting could be provided – a convenience long wished for. In Taddiport villagers were so keen to acquire lights they clubbed together to buy them, and here, in July 1953, we see the culmination of their fund-raising efforts.

We take piped water for granted today, yet in the 1950s many of the smaller villages and hamlets of North Devon were only just getting connected to the mains. Here we see 87-year-old Mrs Blanche Conibear, 'the oldest inhabitant of Marwood', turning on the supply to the hamlets of Prixford, Guineaford and Kingsheanton in February 1952.

As villages were connected up to the electricity grid so the electricity board pushed for greater use in towns. These two photographs from 1950 picture the new showrooms in Combe Martin and Torrington. The poster in the window of the Torrington branch (below) demonstrates the rather simple approach to advertising that was common during that period.

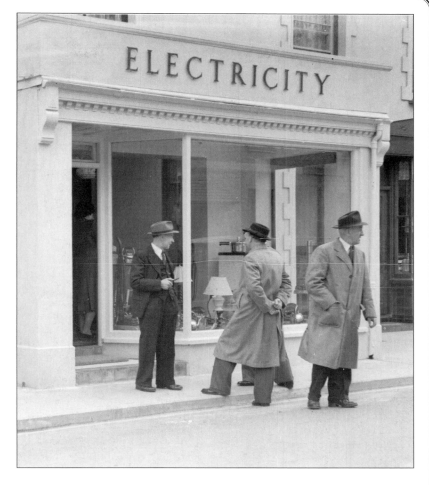

The Victorian Pavilion Theatre in Ilfracombe was built to mark Queen Victoria's Golden Jubilee in 1887 and became very popular with visitors and tourists alike. On 28 June 1949, however, fire broke out at around 1.30p.m. and rapidly consumed the central portion, leaving the two glass wings largely undamaged. Thousands of people lined Capstone to view the conflagration.

Work begun within weeks to repair the damage, although the contractors, W. Woolaway & Son, reckoned that the large degree of structural damage caused to the building meant the work would take some time.

Much of this view of the High Street in Barnstaple is still there, albeit in a much changed form. The three-tiered building (Elliotts) was built in the seventeenth century though the frontage was completely rebuilt in 1971. It now houses an outdoor pursuits shop whilst the shop to the left – Maypole's grocers – is now occupied by Etams. The lane to the right of Elliotts is Holland Lane, now a much more upmarket shopping area than it appears here.

This splendid shot shows the Westminster Bank, Barnstaple in the building now occupied by a café. It is famous for its intricate plaster ceiling, dating from the seventeenth century, and the building is still instantly recognizable today. Both Briggs and Macfisheries (on the far right) have now disappeared.

Barnstaple today is known, not without reason, as the 'Home of the traffic jam', but things were the same, if not worse, in 1952 when these photographs appeared in the *Journal-Herald* to illustrate the new traffic islands built in the Square 'to solve congestion'. At the back is the now demolished building that adjoined the old North Devon Athenaeum.

The Braunton to Barnstaple road, just by Heanton Court, was a notorious blackspot for many years owing to its narrowness and lack of visibility. In 1954, Devon County Council decided to tackle the problem as shown above and by February 1955, when the photograph below was taken, they had made major progress towards completing their improvement scheme.

In 1950 the CEGB began excavating the foundations for a new coal-fired power station at Yelland, on the Taw estuary. Its construction was followed with great interest by locals as it was the largest building in North Devon to that date. The first two generators at the station had been formally commissioned in 1953, and the first coal ship discharged at the newly-built

Yelland quay in that year, as shown in the photograph left. The building was still incomplete and, although the quay was in operation, many of the large components came by rail – as shown in this photograph where a 90-ton transformer is arriving at Barnstaple Junction goods yard on a specially-built bogey in May 1954.

These two photographs give some idea of the scale of construction at Yelland. In July 1951, three 35-ton boilers arrived at the site by rail and were unloaded by a crane normally used by British Rail for righting derailed engines and coaches.

The station was finally opened on 21 April 1955 and cost around £11 million. It was later altered to be oil-fired and finally closed in 1985 when 700 tons of asbestos that had been used in its construction were buried on site. The future of the land is still in question.

In the early 1950s Barnstaple Town Council decided to expand the old cattle market next to the Castle mound. In order to do this they demolished the Victorian 32-cell Borough Gaol in Castle Street. This had a chequered history, having been built in 1874 to replace an older building. Within four years, however, it had become redundant when a new Parliamentary Act meant all long-term prisoners were taken off to Exeter. Following this the gaol was used for a variety of purposes before disappearing in April 1954.

This panoramic view of the Strand in Barnstaple was taken in June 1950 from the Bridge Buildings and, though the scene is still very recognizable today, the uses to which the buildings have been put have changed greatly. The bus station to the left has now been completely altered and traffic has been restricted to a one-way flow. The awful architectural disaster of the Civic Centre had of course yet to be built.

Now a suburb of Barnstaple, Bickington was once a small, self-contained hamlet. A church was built in 1911 but was destroyed by fire some 40 years later. The diocese of Exeter demolished the ruin and cleared the site. These two photographs show the building following the fire and, from May 1955, the vicar helping to complete the new church, which was dedicated to St Paul. It was consecrated in June 1956.

As part of the rebuilding of the Albert (later Queen's) Hall in Barnstaple, following a major fire, this 55-foot-long 10-ton steel girder was eased in through a window in July 1951. It was one of two designed to support the balcony that still exists today.

Along with the external refurbishment, the interior of the Queen's Hall was also brought up to date. The John Gay Tavern was constructed when a spare room was converted into 'one of the most modern bars in North Devon' – this photograph from May 1956 is redolent of the world of 1950s chic – and looks pretty soulless I think!

Now a quiet backwater of bustling Barnstaple, the River Yeo (behind today's Civic Centre) was once a busy river port. This photograph, taken in July 1955, shows two coasters – the *Garlandstone* and the *Emily Barratt*. The large building in the background burnt down in 1966.

Over the next few pages are a selection of views of North Devon towns and villages. All of them display what to us seems an eerie absence of cars. Street lighting is also missing, as are today's ubiquitous double-glazed windows.

The Parish Church of St Michael in Torrington looks serene here but has had a very chequered history. During a Civil War battle in February 1646 about 200 Royalist prisoners were held inside it following the defeat of Lord Hopton by the Puritan Fairfax. Unfortunately, the Puritans also kept their gunpowder stores in the building and for some reason they exploded, killing many and destroying the church. It was substantially rebuilt in 1651 and enthusiastically but drastically 'restored' in 1864.

Looking down Fore Stret in Ilfracombe towards the harbour in 1954. The view is still easily recognizable today although readers will not be surprised to learn that the street is now one-way with limited access.

The main street in Beaford, before the advent of massive car flows and the recent plethora of 'traffic-calming' measures. Designed to slow traffic down, they have been successful – even if they are rather intrusive into the village scene. Beaford today is notable as the headquarters of the Beaford Arts Centre, responsible for taking various art events to the villages of North Devon.

The Woodford Bridge Hotel and Country Club near Holsworthy, pictured in June 1956. This complex of thatched buildings has developed extensively over the years since this view was taken, although the hill in the background has not become any less steep!

This striking juxtaposition of the old and new was taken in West Down in September 1950. The photographer had chatted to the landlord of the Crown, who said the village had three grievances – they had no bus service, no electricity and no sewerage – and the only change over the last 25 years had been the building of just eight new houses!

Taken in May 1952, this shows Croyde's new Post Office, which, according to the contemporary caption, had just been reopened on 'the site of the original post box placed there over 100 years ago'.

These two views of Combe Martin date from August 1950 and were taken at a time when the traditional market gardening the settlement was famous for was giving way to tourism as the main earner. At this date up to 5,000 visitors a week were arriving and traffic congestion was becoming a real problem (nothing new!). There were four chapels, eight public houses and films were screened twice a week in the British Legion Hall.

A group of passers-by stop to pass the time of day outside the new Appledore library in June 1952. Devon County Council still maintain a large number of library premises, supplementing them with mobile library vans which reach even the most isolated of readers.

This charming village is Parracombe. The photograph was taken in 1950 when there were two churches, two chapels, a police station, a pub and a population of 300. The village school was run by Miss Blackmore who had been a pupil, a monitor and a teacher there for some 60 years. Belying the 'chocolate box' image presented here was the fact that at the time all the sewerage from the inhabitants ended up in the village stream – a source of great worry to the locals and a problem that wasn't tackled for some years.

Berrynarbor (above) is one of the prettiest villages in North Devon yet is rather overshadowed (in terms of visitor numbers) by Watermouth Castle, also in the parish. This Gothic house was built circa 1825 and is now operated as a tourist attraction. The photograph captures well some of the serenity and beauty that is still to be found in the village.

These Nissen huts were constructed in Northam for military personnel who worked on the development of secret weapons in the Westward Ho! area during the Second World War. The most famous of these was the 'Panjandrum' – a bizarre exploding wheel designed to roll into coastal defences and demolish them when detonated.

In June 1950 the *Journal-Herald* began an occasional series entitled 'Focus on your village'. The first article dealt with High Bickington and the reporter noted that there was no sewerage, no electricity and no piped water. Additionally, the dustmen only called once a month and buses only went to Barnstaple twice a week. Lighting was by oil lamps and water had to be collected in buckets from the village pump. On a more positive note, the mobile cinema called weekly, about one in seven of the population of 500 belonged to the athletic club, whilst the local pub had both shove ha'penny and darts teams, although apparently 'skittles have dropped out of favour'. Certainly, the main impression from the photographs is of a quiet and very clean village with no cars or litter in sight.

CHAPTER THREE
❧ FARMING ❧

Agriculture has been at the heart of North Devon for centuries and only recently has been supplanted by tourism as the source of the area's main income. Over the last 50 years other changes have affected farming – new crops have been introduced, mechanisation has replaced horses and farm labourers as a group have virtually disappeared. The selection of photographs shown here illustrates a way of life now largely lost to us.

Mr W. Day of Lower Yelland Farm, Fremington admiring two of his prize saddleback sows in February 1952.

Another harvest shot, this time from August 1955 at Landkey.

Fields of wheat and barley were harvested from the edges inwards and as the area of uncut crops grew smaller any rabbits in the field were hemmed in, finally trying to escape in a wild run – often to be met by boys such as these pictured, who caught them for their mothers to prepare for the table. This harvest scene shows a self-binder at work in Westleigh in August 1953 with two boys armed with sticks.

Mechanisation of agriculture was proceeding apace when this photograph was taken in August 1951 at Halmpstone Farm, Bishops Tawton. It shows a combine harvester 'of continental pattern' being used in North Devon for the first time. It was harvesting a 12-acre field of specially grown 'short Maya barley' for the tenant farmer Gerald Stanbury, the operation being 'watched with interest by many agriculturists'.

Codden Hill dominates the skyline near Barnstaple and is a favourite spot for visitors today. Following the war, however, the Devon War Agricultural Committee began pressing for the cultivation of the area to meet Britain's demand for food. A packed public meeting in June 1949 voted 57 to 15 'that Codden Hill remain as it is', but the national need led to part of it being ploughed up, as shown in this photograph.

The foot and mouth outbreak that devastated North Devon and Britain in 2001 is not a new experience for the area's farmers. In August 1953 vets confirmed the existence of the disease at East Anson Farm in Ashreigney. The farmer, F.S. Parfitt, saw his valuable herd of Guernsey cows destroyed and his farm put into quarantine, as this photograph shows. All local animal markets were closed and a 15-mile-radius 'no movement' area designated. Neighbouring Crabden Farm was also affected, but the outbreak was soon brought under control with locals drawing on experience gained from a previous occurrence in 1932 at Combe Martin.

In 1945, Tom Anstey established the Instow Horse and Agricultural Show, which later grew into the still continuing North Devon Show. In the 1950s the Instow Show regularly attracted around 1,000 entries from all over the South West. The picture shows the one held in August 1952, when W.P. Mingo of Whimple won the prize for the 'Best Agricultural Mare or Gelding'.

In 1940, cattle markets were taken under the control of the Government who fixed prices to prevent profiteering and allow the fair rationing of meat. Surprisingly, this control was only lifted in July 1954 and this photograph captures the first free auction in Barnstaple. The auctioneer was C. Southcombe and he sold much livestock below its previously protected high price levels, including 14 lambs which went for £3.18s.0d. (£3.90) each instead of their previously guaranteed price of £5.1s.0d. (£5.05). It was noted unsurprisingly that 'Butchers in the familiar striped aprons were prominent among the buyers.'

Another atmospheric shot, this time from September 1949, shows barley threshing going on at the 500-acre Ash Barton Farm in Braunton. Mr William Isaac (third from the right) was supervising operations for the tenant farmer H.J. Bowden.

This shot shows the lifting of mangolds at an unnamed Goodleigh farm in November 1953. The original caption noted that 'Root crops have been well up to expectation this year.'

Potato planting is not perhaps as photogenic as a harvest scene but the crop was just as important in feeding post-war Britain. Here we see W.E. Day planting early potatoes at his farm in Yelland in March 1955.

Amongst the activities carried out by Young Farmers' Clubs were education and competitions, and here we see a group photograph of those taking part in a Braunton ploughing competition held in December 1953.

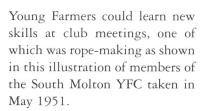

Young Farmers could learn new skills at club meetings, one of which was rope-making as shown in this illustration of members of the South Molton YFC taken in May 1951.

At the same event, aspiring young farmers were being taught how to make spars for use on their farms.

This animated scene, pictured in June 1952, shows judges, timekeepers and spectators watching competitors in the Chittlehampton Young Farmers' Club sheep shearing competition held at Cobbaton.

Even in the 1950s the use of horsepower was declining fast and this beautiful photograph, dating from April 1956, was captioned: 'No longer a common sight this three-horse team is pulling a timber wagon at Filleigh with logs from the Castle Hill estate.' The picture was later used for the free pull-out calendar for 1957, which was issued by the *Journal-Herald*.

This photograph shows George Hawkins passing down a bundle of spars to 69-year-old Jim Hooper at Durdon Farm in Winkleigh in March 1953, where they are apparently finishing off a rick.

Although not heavily wooded, North Devon has for many years produced a variety of timber products, although business has had to adapt to meet changing markets. Here, in an illustration from 1953, we see three workmen on the Stucley estate at North Molton cutting pit-props for the Somerset coal mines – a market that has long since disappeared.

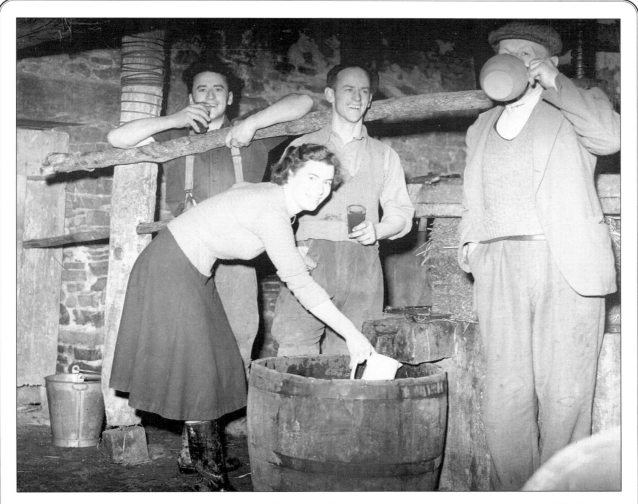

The original caption to this picture reads as follows: 'Cider makers taste the brew! A scene at Wellesleigh Farm, Bishops Tawton where cider making, almost a lost art in the farms, has been in full swing. Mr H.E. Smith senior is drinking from the jug. Pouring is Mrs M. Down, his daughter, and with her are her two brothers, Messrs Ernest and John Smith. The Smiths have farmed Wellesleigh for over 50 years.'

This fine action shot from July 1952 shows Mr D. Morris at Garton Hill Farm, alongside the Torrington to South Molton road, using his pitchfork on top of a load of hay. It clearly demonstrates the amount of sheer human muscle power that was needed to farm in the 1950s.

The Hartland-based blacksmith, Tom Conibear, was said to be still busy even though the number of horses he was asked to shoe was well down. This photograph dates from December 1955. (Tom also appears on p.71)

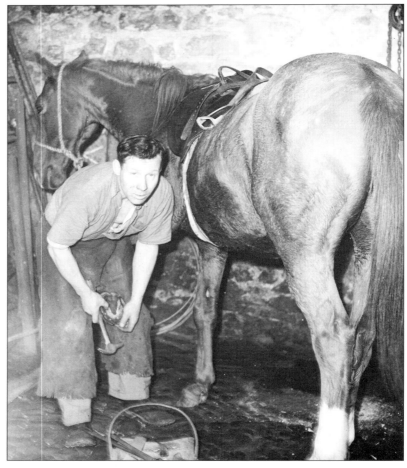

With the number of cattle markets declining rapidly as rationalisation occurs (along with direct purchase of animals by supermarket chains) it is hard to recall that even small communities once had their own markets. Here, from June 1955, we see farmers gathered in the village square in Burrington to buy and sell stock.

Something that is unlikely to ever happen again is pictured here from when Barnstaple staged its first Dairy Show in November 1953. The Pannier Market was floored with straw to make the beasts comfortable – impossible today under modern hygiene regulations. Six breeds were shown and there was even a class for 'the progeny of artificially inseminated animals'. The Torridge Vale Dairy Cup for the best team of three animals went to these Ayrshires, bred by S.J. Woolway of Exeter.

A picture from the South Molton Fat Stock Show of December 1954, when local farmers vied to win the top prizes which guaranteed them the best prices for their animals from butchers stocking up for Christmas. Here we see H.A. Luxton of Oakwell, Kingsnympton with his champion beast.

These two atmospheric shots date from 1954 and show the annual Autumn round-up of Exmoor ponies. Always low in numbers, the breed suffered a catastrophic decline during the Second World War, when the moor was used extensively for military training. Now there are up to around 1,000 in total worldwide and they are left to roam free until being brought in for sale. The *Journal-Herald* recorded that in June 1954 an Exmoor mare and foal were sold in Barnstaple Cattle Market for the handsome price of 30 guineas (£31.50).

CHAPTER FOUR
❧ WORK ❧

The long-established firm of Shapland & Petter won an order in 1949 to construct a new carved oak lantern for the roof of the Middle Temple in London, to replace one destroyed in the blitz. The company's men are seen here putting the 30-foot-high structure together prior to its unveiling by the Queen.

Widespread cattle raising in North Devon led to the growth of a major leather industry and one of the main products was the glove, with Torrington being at the centre of the industry. In February 1953 Thomas Quick of Well Street in Torrington was photographed at work, cutting gloves in the factory of Messrs William Vaughan & Son in the town. He had begun work there aged 11 in 1890 and unsurprisingly was the oldest member of staff when this picture was taken.

The village of Swimbridge can claim two places in the history of work. Its tannery, shown here in 1949, had been operating in the village since around 1700 and in 1884 it was one of the links in the first telephone installed in North Devon when its owners, John and William Smyth, decided to connect their manufactory with their offices in Barnstaple.

Leather from local tanneries went to many local firms for manufacture into finished products such as gloves, and here, in February 1949, we see an employee of the Pilton Glove Works. This company began in around 1855 and by the 1880s was employing some 200 people to produce over 200 styles of glove. Sadly, as fashions changed, the sale of gloves declined and the firm finally closed in 1970.

Gravel and sand working went on for many years on Crow Point at the entrance to the Taw–Torridge estuaries as shown above, but the huge boom in house building in the 1950s created a demand that couldn't be met from this source. To meet it, Messrs Woolaway of Barnstaple, the area's largest building firm, had this specialist vessel built in Holland. Named the *Stan Woolaway,* it lifted sand directly from the sea bed – a source that is now being actively reconsidered in the Bristol Channel.

The two photographs and that opposite, top, show salmon fishermen at Bideford Bridge. Such Devon fisheries are recorded as far back as AD857 and 13 salmon fisheries are recorded in the Domesday Book (1086). The Bideford one was then valued at 25s.0d. (£1.25) a year – the most valuable in Devon. Overfishing in the eighteenth and nineteenth centuries hit the catches and they fell even lower in the late-twentieth century when pollution of the Torridge from modern farming and sewage outfalls affected them. Today they are still in a precarious state and the scenes shown here have long gone.

In 1874 the Torridge Vale butter factory was set up to process locally-produced milk. Seen as a vital part of the North Devon agricultural economy, its closure came as a massive blow to Torrington; a disaster from which the town is still recovering even today. This photograph gives some idea of the importance of the factory with its impressive line-up of milk-collection lorries dating from a period when milk was collected in churns not tankers – a practice only abandoned in 1979.

Taken around July 1951 on Appledore quay, this picture shows a group of local people mending nets, although in this instance the village postman seems to have joined in as well – probably to chat and swop stories.

Snapped on the quay at Appledore in May 1954, this photograph shows 14-year-old Rosemary Fishwick and her father Tom, a Trinity House pilot, mending fishing nets along with Victor Keen. It was thought that she was the youngest girl to mend nets in North Devon – which suggests that there must have been quite a few other females doing the job.

Before the widespread use of plastics the humble basket was a much valued item in everyday life. The making of such things was carried on in every area where the withies could be grown and here we see George Mock of Mill Style, Braunton in December 1952 making a basket. He had been producing them for nearly 60 years and his baskets 'had gone all over the world.'

The old world of agriculture had many associated trades, one of the most obvious being the blacksmith. Even in the 1950s, however, the trade was declining and this photograph shows William Wright of South Molton in January 1953. Owing to the shortage of smiths he also operated forges in Kingsnympton and North Molton.

One of Bideford and North Devon's most famous contemporary potters is Harry Juniper, who produces superb work that harks back to the slip-ware produced in the area in the seventeenth century. To prove the truism that everyone has to start somewhere, he is seen here in July 1951 placing one of his entries in the pottery show of the Bideford Art School Summer Exhibition. The building itself still survives but the school disappeared some years ago and is still badly missed by many in the town.

North Devon's most famous painter Reg Lloyd snapped in Bideford Pannier Market in 1956. Reg arrived in Bideford in 1956 and still lives there. His work is represented in the Tate, the National Maritime Museum and the Victoria and Albert amongst other places. The lady in the photogarph is Miss Jeffery who came from Weare Giffard and was the last stallholder who brought her produce in by pony and trap!

Amongst the glories of North Devon are its pannier markets in Barnstaple, Bideford and South Molton. Sadly the imposition of new health regulations has meant that sights such as this have now been consigned to history. Taken in Barnstaple's market in April 1953, it shows a Mrs Hubber of Hearson Farm in Swimbridge serving real Devonshire cream to seven-year-old Annette Parkin and her grandmother.

This smiling group features 11-year-old Marjorie Hosegood of Witheridge, the champion butter maker of the Bath and West Show held at Exeter in June 1954. She lived at Bradford Barton Farm and went to Chulmleigh School. Apparently she didn't just make butter on her parents' farm but also drove a tractor, whitewashed the shippens, trimmed hedges and painted the farm implements.

In the 1980s, serious concerns were raised about the falling catches of fish in the River Torridge, which was famous amongst fishermen for its salmon. Pollution from modern farming methods was affecting stocks and although the situation has improved in recent years one wonders if we will ever see a scene like this again. Dating from April 1956, it shows an elver trap constructed at Beam Weir just outside of Torrington for the Devon Rivers Board. Elvers are small eels.

Navigation up the River Taw to Barnstaple became increasingly difficult in the eighteenth and nineteenth centuries and thus in August 1848 the small quay at Fremington was linked to Barnstaple by a horse drawn railway to turn the village into a type of outport. Seven years later steam trains took over and the original 'lifting bridge' was replaced with an iron bridge in 1880. As ships became larger, so Fremington quay declined and by the 1950s when this shot was taken only coal was being imported with ball clay being exported.

This jolly looking postman is William 'Bob' Mitchell of Georgenympton. Aged 67 when this photograph was taken in July 1956, he had to cover an 11-mile delivery route around South Molton daily and began using his two ponies, 'Miss Maud' and 'Dolly', in the very cold winter of 1947 when snow caused major problems in getting around.

Recently reintroduced by Devon County Council, lengthmen such as the gentleman photographed here had the job of keeping the roads clean, clearing gutters and drains, trimming back hedges and tidying grass verges. Each worked a separate area and the Braunton district, for example, had nine of them. The man shown here is John Davey who, it was reported, took such a pride in his work that he made all his own tools.

This elderly gentleman, pictured working so intently in his crowded workshop in 1951, was Frank Gaydon. His watchmaking business was based at 6 The Strand, Barnstaple and over his long life (1863–1956) he had repaired tens of thousands of timepieces. He had followed his father John (1821–95) into the business and between them they had well over a century's experience. His family presented the church clock at Swimbridge.

Here we see W.J. Tapp, the village blacksmith of Bishopsnympton, standing at the door of his forge with one of his customers, called 'Twilight'. Apparently he served a wide area, which included Molland, Rose Ash and Anstey as well as Bishopsnympton, and had modern ideas – as the *Journal-Herald* reported, 'electricity is used to work his bellows and to help him in many other ways.'

These two pictures record scenes from the Bideford Festival Trades Exhibition held at the town's sports ground over the period of 11–16 June 1951. This was part of the national Festival of Britain and was designed to be a showcase for local manufacturers. During the week the Bideford Silver Band put on two concerts and there was a 'Mannequin Parade', a Baby Show (won by Susan Andrew), and an 'Agricultural Any Questions' panel. A 'Homecraft' show attracted 400 entries with a Mrs Seldon winning the 'Knitted Socks' event and a Mrs Henson triumphing as the the victor in the 'Bottling in Syrup' competition.

The shipyard of P.K. Harris at Appledore turned out a whole succession of sturdy vessels in the 1950s and here we see the *Sydney Cove* after completion, just before she was setting out to go to Australia in May 1956. P.K. Harris is seen with his men taking a last look over her before she sailed from Appledore quay.

Seen here with some of her crew is the schooner *Result,* a coasting vessel well known in North Devon 50 years ago. During the First World War she had been a 'Q' ship, successfully engaging two U-boats. But by 1950, when these pictures were taken, she was being refitted at Appledore to her original square rig in order to take part in the filming of Conrad's 'Outcast of the Islands'. Captain P. Balsh of Braunton had as his bosun R. Lamey of Appledore, with his quartermaster being T. Slade, also from Appledore. There were four other crew members plus the ship's dog 'Mark'.

Pilton is the oldest part of Barnstaple and when, in August 1951, the *Journal-Herald* printed this picture of 91-year-old John Frayne it asked the question 'is this the oldest cabinet maker in the country?' John lived at 113 Pilton Street and was said to be 'a true craftsman' in that 'he scorns the use of a nail'.

This picture, with its echoes of Russian posters of heroic workers, shows Mr and Mrs S.W. Springall of Taunton, who were working for the Barnstaple Brick and Tile Co., tiling a roof in Chaddiford Lane, Barnstaple. Mrs Springall, who had a nine-year-old son, was believed to be the only female tiler in England. She was noted as being 'a remarkably dexterous worker' whilst he 'carried the tiles, balanced on his head, from ground to roof.'

In the digital age, such scenes as this look positively prehistoric. The photograph was actually taken in March 1957 to show Marina Horne, a 21-year-old South Molton telephone operator, who was emigrating to Canada. The photographer, however, has also recorded the hand-operated trunk dialling system then used to connect long-distance telephone calls. With the virtual disappearance of human telephone operators the picture is a valuable record of vanished technology.

This group photograph shows the staff of the Barnstaple Food Office in 1951. Set up to run the rationing system during the war they continued working for some years after the conflict when shortages meant rationing remained in place. I still have my own sweets ration book dating from 1953.

The Braund family of Bucks Mills has long been famous in the area and this charming shot shows 80-year-old Ernest Braund making baskets in January 1948. Whilst having his portrait taken he recalled how Bucks Mills once had 16 fishing boats with 32 crew who fished during the winter months and 'went to sea in the Merchant service during the summer.'

Not many films have been made in North Devon, but in October 1956 the J. Arthur Rank Organisation came to Hele Beach in Ilfracombe to film scenes from *High Tide at Noon* starring Betta St John and Michael Craig.

Donkeys at Clovelly being shod by Hartland blacksmith Tom Conibear, who had learned his craft whilst on Army service in Italy. He had been doing the Clovelly work for some time when this picture was taken in September 1953. It was noted that the donkeys needed re-shoeing every three to four weeks owing to the wear they experienced on the rough Clovelly cobbles.

Although the cobbles were picturesque, weeding them was a thankless task and here we see villagers doing the job. Sweeping the cobbles is Bill Headon, the 'scavenger' employed by Devon County Council, who was not allowed to help under the rules of his job.

The streets of post-war Britain were thronged with tradesmen of all description – the Corona lemonade vans, the fruit and veg carts, French onion men and the scissor sharpener. Pictured here in May 1955 is Tex Taylor, 'one of a long line of Barnstaple tinkers with his workshop on wheels.' He was plying his trade in Park Lane in Bideford and told the reporter who interviewed him that his biggest problem was 'a traffic one – controlling the numbers of children who love to watch him at work.'

Having mentioned the door to door fruit and veg sellers, here is Mr E. Corke on his rounds in Appledore in April 1953. His cart was pulled by 12-year-old 'Dolly' who was a great favourite with the children.

Appledore quay was long famous as a busy place for incoming and outgoing cargoes, but as ships became larger and problems with silting developed trade declined and thus, in April 1954, the *Journal-Herald* thought it unusual enough to picture the *mv Irene* discharging animal feed at the village quay. The report noted that she was only the second ship to discharge at the quay since 1945. Clearly, the harbourmaster, Captain J. Hobbs, wasn't rushed off his feet!

Another cargo arrived in February 1955, this time consisting of oyster shells which rather bizarrely were being brought in to feed local poultry.

This shot, though clearly posed, is charming and shows 'Appledore's flower seller', Mrs Mary Hardtke, who grew all her stock in her garden, standing on her doorstep in June 1953 whilst Mrs Florence Guegan is making a purchase.

A long-established tradition, now sadly lost, was the unloading and selling of fish direct from the fishing boats on Bideford quay. Both visitors and locals alike gathered around whenever the boats came home. This was the scene one day in June 1953.

This fine-looking old gentleman was 80-year-old Fred Richards of the Old Almshouses, St Giles in the Wood. Pictured in February 1956 he could claim to have been making violins for 62 years. Born in St Giles, he had spent his working life as a carpenter on the Rolle estate and became interested in making musical instruments when Lady Gertrude Rolle brought a craftsman from the London Arts and Industries Association to hold classes in the village. Incidentally, Fred had used the same handsaw for his entire career!

This skilled gunmaker was Mr R.W. Turvey of Barnstaple who was carrying on a family tradition; his forefathers had worked in the same trade for 200 years. When pictured in January 1953, Mr Turvey had already been working in the trade for 22 years.

CHAPTER FIVE

PUBLIC SERVICES

In the 1940s the Devon police force expanded its number of women officers and here, from October 1949, we see the two based in Barnstaple. P.W.E. Taylor had arrived in 1944 after serving in the Wiltshire Womens' Auxiliary Police Force, whilst P.W. Mavis Stableforth had just joined after working as a clerk for the Ministry of Food at Axminster.

Here we see Romeo Berry, Mayor of Barnstaple, inaugurating the 999 emergency telephone system at the end of February 1946. Unfortunately for the Mayor, only minutes before he was due to place his ceremonial call to the local police and fire brigade, a real emergency call came in and he had to be content to be second best. Incidentally, when he did place his call a police car arrived on the spot in 20 seconds!

In 1949 North Devon members of the National Fire Service gathered in Barnstaple to take part in an intensive month's training, which included work on the turntable ladder and with the new foam-spreading equipment, used to quench fires.

The Ilfracombe Fire Brigade pose proudly on their engine some time around 1949–50, possibly just after fighting the Victoria Pavilion fire.

Training was always important and here the Barnstaple engine is seen at a practice in Boutport Street where they attended a simulated emergency in the Gaumont Theatre before an appreciative audience.

The NALGO holiday camp at Croyde Bay is still in being today, having been built in the 1930s. Closed for the duration of the war it was reopened in May 1947 with a celebratory dance. Two hours after the dance finished smoke was seen issuing from the dancehall and within a short time it was completely destroyed, notwithstanding the best efforts of the Braunton, Barnstaple and Ilfracombe fire brigades.

The village of Appledore has long been famous for its ships and shipbuilding skills. During the war the yard of P.K. Harris did sterling work, but in June 1947 a disastrous fire hit the yard and within a year another fire destroyed even more of the premises. This photograph dates from the May 1948 conflagration when a machine shop, power unit and a rigging store were consumed. Fire brigades from Appledore, Bideford and Barnstaple attended but couldn't stem the flames, although they did save a tug lying in the dry dock which was on fire at one point.

In September 1956 a fire broke out in Buller Road, Barnstaple and although quickly brought under control a garage, hardware store and blacksmith's shop were extensively damaged.

Barnstaple Junction Station at the bottom of Sticklepath Hill was a major part of the transport system in this part of Devon and, as befits its status, had a large house provided for the stationmaster. On one Monday morning in March 1956 smoke was seen coming from the roof and the railway fire brigade began to tackle the blaze, being quickly joined by the town brigade. Although two bedrooms were gutted the stationmaster's three pedigree whippets were rescued. The building still stands today but has been empty for some years.

This dramatic illustration from March 1953 shows the after-effects of a destructive fire at the seventeenth-century Coach and Horses pub at Swimbridge. The fire began in a chimney at the east end of the inn and in a strong wind rapidly spread. The village policeman, PC Grimmett, tackled it with a stirrup pump until the arrival of the Barnstaple Fire Brigade and eventually their efforts were successful, but not before much damage was caused. Local volunteers helped remove the thatch from the roof using pitchforks and a tractor was used to dump it in nearby fields.

All in a day's work for the men of the Barnstaple Fire Brigade. This small fire occurred in the North Devon Infirmary in 1949. Luckily the blaze was soon brought under control and no real lasting damage was done.

Not many villages could boast their own fire crews but Hartland was one of them and here we see members overhauling their equipment in October 1955.

The present-day ATTURM (Amphibious Trials and Training Unit Royal Marines) camp at Instow can trace its origins back to the Second World War beach-landing practices that were carried out along this part of the coast. Training and experiments have been carried on ever since, as these pictures from July 1950 show.

The use of nuclear weapons at the end of the Second World War ushered in a period of mutual antagonism between the capitalist and communist blocs. To meet the perceived threat from Russia and its allies the Government established the Civil Defence, which, in hindsight, appears to have been a rather 'Dad's Army' type of organisation. In this photograph from April 1954 we see Captain H. Hallett, the area CD officer, and Police Sergeant Clinnick testing some newly-received 'Radiac' instruments, which measured levels of radioactivity 'after an atomic bomb explosion' – although one wonders why survivors would have bothered.

Civil Defence instructors travelled widely through North Devon teaching local groups how to prepare for survival following a nuclear war. One of these was Mrs J. Lennard, a Women's Voluntary Service member of Chulmleigh Civil Defence Unit, who is seen here superintending the building of a field kitchen at Chulmleigh. Apparently 'hot dogs' were on the menu.

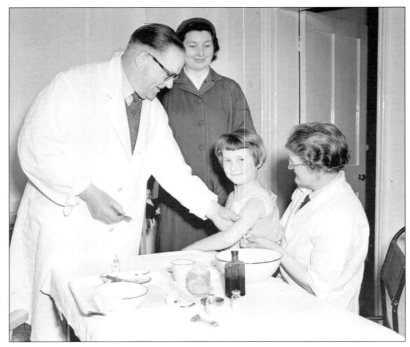

During the period covered by this book the crippling disease, polio, became a major worry for parents all over England following serious outbreaks, including one in North Devon. The new National Health Service instituted a mass-vaccination campaign against the disease and here, from May 1956, we see one of the first children in Barnstaple to be injected with the new anti-polio vaccine. The campaign was extremely successful and paved the way for many others.

North Devon boasts many old cottages built of cob, which over time falls prey to harsh weather conditions. In January 1955, however, a Southern National double-decker rolled some 60 feet into the cob front of Mayleigh Cottage at Georgeham with the results seen below. Mrs Minnie Boucher, who was in her front room when the bus came through the wall, was miraculously unhurt, though badly shocked. Here the Croyde constable, PC F. Brook, stands by the wreckage.

The Kenwith Valley in Bideford has had a long history of flooding and hopefully scenes like this, from January 1955, should be a thing of the past. This particular occasion was said to be the worst for ten years. The alarm had been sounded by a local resident at 6a.m. and although the Bideford Fire Brigade was quickly on the scene with three pumps, some 14 houses were flooded.

This shot shows the crowds who gathered to see the naming ceremony of the new Ilfracombe lifeboat, the *Robert and Phemian Brown*, in August 1953. Robert was a Scottish sea captain from Fife who owed his life to the RNLI and purchased the boat as a 'debt of gratitude'. It was 36' long, had a beam of 10' 8" and weighed 8.5 tons fully laden.

In 1899 during a blizzard the Lynmouth lifeboat was hauled by horses over Countisbury and Exmoor to be launched at Porlock where a schooner, the *Forest Hall*, was in distress. By December 1948 when this photograph was taken only two of the original crew members were still living – Captain George Richards and William Richards. This photograph shows, from left: William Richards, T. Bevan, E. Pedder and Captain George Richards.

These shots show the naming ceremony of the *William Cantrell Ashley* lifeboat in Clovelly on 27 June 1950. The 35.5' 'Liverpool' type boat had arrived in the village some nine months earlier, after having been constructed at Cowes using a legacy from Charles Ashley of Mentone in France. She replaced the *City of Nottingham* boat. She was named by the Countess Fortescue who attended, along with the Royal Marine band.

In September 1949 local members of the newly-formed Territorial Army went to Withypool to help restore the famous 'Clapper Bridge' at Tarr Steps as part of their training. One aspect of this was the erection of this suspension bridge, shown left and below.

This striking photograph records the burial at sea of Cpl David Ward of the Royal Electrical and Mechanical Engineers. He had been attached to the 34th Amphibious Support Regiment at Braunton and drowned when his vehicle floundered on Barnstaple Bar on 2 April 1947. His body was found a month later and taken from Appledore to be consigned to the sea some five miles offshore. As the boat carrying the body left Appledore it is recorded that all the workmen in the shipyard there bared their heads.

Following the war many communities added names to their First World War memorials. Braunton went one better and opened a war memorial garden. Here, in May 1951, we see E.J. Slee, the former Chairman of the Parish Council, who had been instrumental in getting the scheme up and running, at the opening ceremony.

Remembrance Day has always been an important occasion in North Devon and this picture shows the Field of Remembrance on Bideford Quay in November 1956. The gentleman in the picture is Ray Wilson, who as an ex-Royal Artillery man is seen with his daughter and her two friends from Northam adding their crosses.

In the 1950s there were still enough First World War veterans to stage large rallies. Here, in October 1953, we see the North Devon members of the 'Old Contemptibles' parading to Barnstaple Parish Church on Sunday, headed by the local British Legion band.

From one war to another. In the first years of the 1950s the Korean War was being fought with the British Army well to the fore. Amongst the prisoners captured by the Communist North Koreans was Monty Cawsey of Bideford. Held captive for 18 months, he was repatriated in October 1953 and was met at Bideford railway station by a cheering crowd, hundreds strong. Asked about his treatment he reported that he 'had to attend compulsory lectures where they were forced to listen to Communist propaganda', which he reckoned 'was a lot of twaddle'.

In the immediate post-war years the British Legion became a major social focus in the area and here in October 1951 we see 18 local standard-bearers leading the South Molton carnival procession that year.

These capable-looking young men were members of the Bideford Sea Scouts, exercising with a handy-looking gun on their training ship called the *Revenge,* under the command of T. Rowe in February 1952.

In September 1951 the various North Devon groups of the St John's Ambulance Brigade held a massive parade in Barnstaple. The different contingents shown here were inspected by Lieutenant General Sir Otto Lund, the UK Commissioner in Chief, and his deputy Lady Brecknock. In his speech he emphasised that the National Health Act (passed several years earlier) 'had by no means decreased the need for voluntary service'.

Bideford Town Council was established in 1832 but its members had no robes until 1951, when local benefactor A. McTaggart Short purchased a set for them. They are seen here being worn for the first time in April 1951 by councillors on their way to St Mary's Church for the special service that is still held on the day following the annual Manor Court ceremony, when the Council, as lords of the manor, meet to hear submissions from the public about the needs of the town.

This group photograph shows some volunteers off to clean up oil pollution on Woolacombe Beach in July 1951. The problem was so bad in the North Devon area that a delegation of four local MPs had gone to the Ministry of Transport to demand action, whilst the Woolacombe and Mortehoe Chamber of Commerce had 'pointed out the seriousness of the position and had stated that every hotelier, without exception, had received serious complaints from visitors, as well as damage to their furnishings, from tar and oil.' They were also angry that no compensation was payable to local councils who had to tackle the problem.

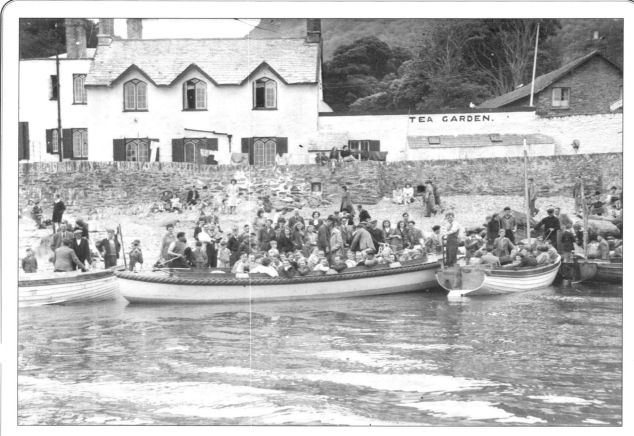

For many years, Lynmouth was a major port of call for steamers bringing day-trippers from South Wales. These were halted during the war, but the first post-war arrival was P. & A. Campbell's *Cardiff Queen* in June 1949. Lynmouth was *en fete* and the Council Chairman, S.C. Willshire, went to meet the tourists saying that he 'was deeply gratified at the recommencement of a service which would be of great benefit to Lynton and Lynmouth. All they wanted now was fine weather and plenty of people.'

CHAPTER SIX

❧ AMUSEMENTS ❧

Barnstaple Fair has been an annual high spot for both children and adults alike for many hundreds of years. Originally an occasion for selling and buying farm animals with a small amusement fair attached, the former has shrunk to disappearance today, whilst the latter has become the main event by far. Here, in these photographs, we see some of the rides brought to Barnstaple in the post-war years when Tom Whitelegg was in charge.

Amongst the attractions at Barnstaple Fair in the 1950s were the 'human curiosities' and below we see an unnamed midget on top of a fair lorry in September 1953. The fair organiser, Tom Whitelegg, was reported as bemoaning the decline in visitors, owing to the impact of television and of people travelling to London to see the coronation. At this date the fair was still held in North Walk and Tom added that 'Although North Walk is the worst fairground I know for entrances and exits, I would not like to see it changed.' It was later moved, of course, and is now to be found near the Leisure Centre.

In the 1950s every town and village in North Devon seemed to be putting on carnivals and fêtes on a regular basis and the photographs taken of these reveal many vignettes of life in those post-war years. Typical of these was the one associated with the Appledore Regatta which, in July 1954, saw the election of Miss Sylvia Passmore of Barnstaple as 'Queen' with four attendants – Hester Sanders, Elizabeth Branch, June Pike and Sheila Pascoe. As befits a Regatta Queen, Sylvia was carried in a specially-decorated boat manned by Harold Stevens, W. Powe and Ian Cox.

This event was the Landkey Methodist Fête, held on Wednesday, 4 June 1952. Organised by Jack Slee, it was opened by the Mayoress of Barnstaple, Mrs J.B. Cruse, in her last public engagement before standing down from office.

The Womens' Institute was usually the main organisation for women in rural areas and here, in July 1954, we see members of the Littleham WI 'casting a critical eye over one of the egg entries at their annual flower show.'

Before the advent of car boot sales, jumble sales were the main way in which people passed on unwanted items to others. The *Journal-Herald* often featured photographs of these events, such as this one from January 1955 which shows the event held by the Barnstaple Amateur Football Club Supporters' Club in an effort to raise funds.

The small village of Westleigh hit the headlines a few years ago when its fête was visited by 'Lady Godiva' on horseback – complete with long hair to protect her modesty. The fête in July 1953 was clearly a more sober affair if this picture is anything to go by.

This definitely politically-incorrect picture was taken at the South Molton Conservative Fête in July 1956. It shows the 'Mousey-Housey' game which involved the stallholder dropping a live mouse onto a table with a series of exit holes, with spectators betting on which hole the hapless mouse would choose! One can only imagine the uproar this would cause today.

Carnival tableaux have often reflected contemporary events and these photographs show some of the events that caught people's attention in the 1950s. This one dates from July 1955, when a flying saucer 'complete with spaceman pilot Stephen Griffin' won first prize in the 'Decorated Small Vehicles Class' at Combe Martin Carnival. The original report notes that the float was 'most appropriate in view of this week's American announcement' – although what this was I have been unable to discover.

The rather odd-looking character in the photo on the left was R. Huxtable, snapped at the June 1953 Brayford Carnival when he was collecting donations for a 'Television set for the village hall' – a reminder of how scarce early sets were in North Devon.

A few months later in the same year the South Molton Carnival had 17 floats, including this entry from Lynton which caused 'a lot of amusement' but threw 'no further light on the Burgess-McLean mystery.' The two gentlemen are dressed as Russian spies, unmasked after working in the British Foreign Office. The float, however, won no prizes even though the carnival itself 'gave the borough its brightest, noisiest and gayest Saturday night on record.'

Bickington held its village fair in May 1951 and it attracted a good crowd. Among the stalls was one where you could purchase a helium-filled balloon with a label attached, on which you could write your name. The prize went to the one that went the furthest (and whose label was returned!). Graham Parkin seems to have won with his balloon ending up in Guildford, Surrey.

One of the most popular carnival events with spectators was the 'Knobbly Knees' contest. At this one from Combe Martin in July 1953 it was noted that it 'drew a lot of support but only from visitors.' Judging was by Carnival Queen Kathleen Cutcliffe who awarded the winning prize to R. Hemstock of London, with H. Martin of London and W. Butler of Hemel Hempstead as runners up.

As television spread its influence in the 1950s, so it became the subject of carnival tableaux. This one, showing Andy Pandy, dates from October 1953 when the South Molton Girl's Training Corps entered 'GTC Television' into the local carnival. It won and its creators were photographed for posterity; they included Mrs V. Cross, Misses J. and D. Holland, V. Burnett, J. Bodley, J. and V. Dymond, W. Denis, M. Horne, G. Boucher, R. Barton and M. Harris.

Now perceived as not 'politically correct', beauty competitions were extremely popular in the 1950s and local photographers enjoyed them as much as anyone else. Here we see the entrants to the 'Belle of the Beach' competition at Ilfracombe in August 1951. No bikinis yet of course!

The 'stage' is rather makeshift but it was all smiles for the camera at the 1955 Combe Martin Carnival beauty contest. The eventual winner was No.4, Miss Gillian Latham, who, it was noted, was an 'Amazon footballer'.

Not all carnivals were blessed with good weather and in August 1954 (below) Miss Combe Martin, Margaret Jones, and her attendants 'found their bathing costumes hardly warm enough for the sort of weather the carnival experienced' – indeed they were soaked through.

The high point of Barnstaple Carnival has always been the choice of the Queen and in 1951 the honour fell to Anita Tucker, a 20-year-old brunette from Braunton. Her attendants were Shirley Brown of Fremington, Margaret Wills and Pat Smith of Barnstaple, and Winnie Smith of Marwood. The *Journal-Herald* thought it worth noting that three married women took part in the contest – evidently not the done thing!

Occasionally North Devon was visited by the ever popular travelling circus and this illustration shows elephants from the Bertram Mills Circus processing through Barnstaple one Sunday afternoon – bearing 'safety first' slogans. Both the Mayor and the Police Superintendant visited the Rock Park Sports Ground to welcome the circus people, only to have one of the performers pick their pockets! The attraction was such that Barnstaple's population was doubled, for 'a long procession of coaches have been shuttling visitors into the town.' The circus itself needed five special trains to bring its livestock and equipment to North Devon.

Torrington May Fair is a notable feature of the events calendar in North Devon and in 1954 the townspeople celebrated the 400th anniversary of the granting of the May Fair Charter. One of the central events of the day has always been the crowning of the May Queen and on this occasion ten-year-old Wendy Smalldon was accorded the honour – an event recorded by the BBC for its national programme.

Two years earlier and the scenes were similar, although in this case the May Queen (left) was Marion Squires, who can be seen being presented to the Mayor, R.M. Boyer.

After the crowning and the speeches the civic party and townspeople began 'floral dancing' to the music of the Torrington Voluntary Silver Band.

The Town Band (right) also played through the town's streets, as shown in the accompanying photograph.

At the same time a Fair and Show was held in the town, although in 1954 it was noted that only one horse was offered for sale; its owner, a Yarnscombe farmer, reckoning that 'in future he intends to rent a tractor' – changing times for sure.

Before The Beatles came the skifflers. Following the lead of Lonnie Donegan young men all over Britain decided that they too could produce music – and using a variety of instruments they did (or at least tried). In March 1957 the Bideford-based 'sextette of skifflers', called The Hound Dogs, played their first date at East-the-Water. Their instruments included a home-made tea-chest bass and, rather bizarrely, two accordions. From left to right, they were Alex Curtis, Bill Stoneman, Ken Tryon, Ron Burrage, Cyril Cox and Bill Berners.

This wonderfully atmospheric picture from July 1957 shows a skiffler surrounded by his adoring fans. He was Senior Aircraftsmen John Taylor, who was based at RAF Chivenor. According to the *Journal-Herald,* his 'teenage followers' had named him 'North Devon's King of Rock'!

As part of the Torrington May Fair in 1953 a pram race was held. Eight local pubs entered teams who had to navigate a course from the Railway Hotel to Barley Grove which included eight 'obstacles', such as stopping at a pub to drink beer through a straw. Here, from April, we see one of the teams putting the finishing touches to their entry.

With all the babies being born in the post-war years, 'baby shows' became a common event at village fêtes. In July 1956 such a show was held at Abbotsham as part of the annual fête. It was opened by a Mrs E. Flint with a rousing speech which included the following: 'The strength of England and its very soul was bound up with the consistent and truly English atmosphere of small Christian communities.' The judges for the baby show were Mesdames Westward and Patterson, but the *Journal-Herald* did not report who had won — do they recognise themselves today I wonder?

Ronald Duncan was a resident of North Devon who, in 1953, put on the Taw and Torridge Festival, which was a week-long 'Festival of the Arts' held in both Bideford and Barnstaple. Among its many highlights were performances by the Humphrey Lyttelton Jazz band, lectures by Henry Williamson and A.G. Street and *The Beggar's Opera* by Benjamin Britten, which starred Peter Pears as Captain Macheath. A handsome programme was produced which contained the map on page 4, drawn by the famous Bideford calligrapher Sheila Hutchinson. Duncan's own play, *Don Juan*, was produced in Bideford with stage settings and costumes by the famous Feliks Topolski. Here is Ronald outside his house in Welcombe.

Another feature of the week was the Festival Fashion Parade in Barnstaple's Queen's Hall, which was compered by Audrey Siddeley from *Vogue* magazine and saw local models displaying clothes by Dior, Balmain and Jean Pateau.

RAF Chivenor had been established in the early years of the war as a base for Atlantic air patrols. Following hostilities it stayed open and its annual 'Air Days' were a great draw for local people. These photographs date from September 1950 and the one below shows a young boy looking at a Meteor jet. Although the event was held in a gale the crowds enjoyed seeing Spitfires, Meteors, Vampires, Beaufighters and Prentice trainers both in the air and on the ground.

CHAPTER SEVEN
❧ ROYALTY ❧

The first post-war visit by royalty to North Devon came in November 1946 when the then Princess Elizabeth stayed at Castle Hill, Filleigh for one night with Lord and Lady Fortescue. She had been at Exeter during the day and, travelling to Castle Hill, found the Devon lanes lined with cheering schoolchildren. The group photograph shows the Princess flanked by her hosts, plus Lady Margaret Fortescue and Lady Elizabeth Baxendale. Standing are the Hon Mrs Elphinstone (a lady in waiting), Lord Fairfax, Captain Baxendale, Lord Tweedsmuir and Mr Burdenell-Bruce. The more informal photographs below were taken on the terrace of Castle Hill.

The death of King George VI in February 1952 was announced to the public by the Town Clerks of the various boroughs in North Devon. In Barnstaple, F.J. Broad, accompanied by the Mayor and Corporation, recalled the 'memory of a life devoted to the call of duty – a king and an English gentleman.' After a period of silence a trumpet fanfare sounded and the clerk proclaimed the accession of Queen Elizabeth II.

In Lynton, the Town Council attended a special church service and here we see the councillors, led by North Devon's only female chairman, Mrs S.W. Slater.

The coronation of Elizabeth II in 1953 led to a huge number of street parties all over the country, which saw an outpouring of joy not witnessed since the end of the war eight years earlier.

The party held by the residents of John Gay Road in Barnstaple was staged in the local Territorial Army Hall and here we see Mrs W.H. Wilkey cutting the large cake, specially baked for the occasion.

In Ilfracombe a more lasting monument to the happy day was created – a bird-bath of Cornish granite. It was presented by the Guides and Brownies of Ilfracombe and was inaugurated by Shirley Matheson pouring water into it for the first time. The local vicar, Revd A.S. Chandler, blessed the bath which was officially received for the town by the Council Chairman, H.P. Smith.

Another coronation tea – this time the one held at Gloster Road in Barnstaple.

As with other coronations in the twentieth century, celebratory mugs were produced and here is the Mayor of Barnstaple, Councillor Dark, presenting the mugs to boys of the town's Grammar School – I wonder how many of these fragile china mementoes still survive?

Barnstaple wasn't the only settlement to mark the happy occasion with the distribution of mugs. This happy group of youngsters brandishing their mugs was snapped at Lynton, where the Council had splashed out to mark the day.

In South Molton a Coronation Fancy Dress competition was held in Hugh Squier Avenue and here we see some of the varied entrants.

In Bideford the Council erected decorations all along the quayside and here we see some of those flags and bunting going up.

Even the tiniest streets were decorated and none came much smaller than Union Street off Allhalland Street, here seen bedecked with bunting.

Union Street in Barnstaple, although in a poor area, went to town with its decorations in order to try to win a competition arranged by the Town Council. Nearby, New Buildings won by decorating the road surfaces as well as the houses. The whole area around Vicarage Street was noted as being 'most heavily decorated'.

Television was still a rarity amongst ordinary house-holders and when one was made available for the public to view the coronation, crowds rapidly gathered. Here we see a captivated group watching the events on television at an unnamed location in Barnstaple.

These two photographs show some of the celebrations held in Braunton. The top one was taken at the Barton Close coronation tea and the bottom one shows a similar tea held in Field Close, where the audience is being entertained by a magician.

In May 1956 Queen Elizabeth II and the Duke of Edinburgh visited Barnstaple and their visit was captured in a long series of photographs of which the following six show some of the highpoints.

In the first we see the Lord Lieutenant of Devon, Earl Fortescue, meeting her at Barnstaple railway station where she arrived at precisely 10a.m. Apparently, just before this picture was taken an unnamed official managed to open the wrong door, but his gaffe was soon forgotten as the Queen travelled to the Guildhall through huge cheering crowds – which included 5,000 children in the Pannier Market.

At the Guildhall the royal couple took to a stage decorated with a 'Cross of St George' made up of 1,500 tulip heads.

Here, various presentations were made with the Queen signing the visitors' book.

Leaving via a heavily-decorated doorway she inspected a Guard of Honour before leaving – a short visit that will be recalled by many still alive today. A controversy developed after the visit about the cost to the town (some 600 yards of material swathed the station roof, for example), but for most people the day was seen as a real red-letter one during which post-war austerity could be forgotten for a while.

CHAPTER EIGHT
❧ LUNDY ❧

In 1949 Arthur Dennis, a local sanitary inspector and a member of the Lundy Field Society, helped by boys from Bryanston School, used large amounts of poison to decimate the rat population of the island, which had been seriously reducing the numbers of nesting birds. The *Journal-Herald* took these photographs at the time but didn't use them, so they appear here for the first time.

Looking up a small valley on the island's plateau top towards Millcombe House. Constructed by the Revd H.G. Heaven when he owned the island it appears rather submerged in vegetation with its gardens choked with rhododendron bushes. It was rebuilt in 1972 and its copper roof restored.

Looking down from the island to the South Light and adjoining Rat Island, just next to the main landing beach. The break between the two islands is known as Hell's Gates.

The Old Lighthouse was built in 1819 to try to cut down the horrifying number of ships wrecked on the dangerous rocks around the island. Unfortunately, according to legend, it was built so high that its light was frequently obscured by cloud! It was taken out of service in 1896 on completion of the North and South Lighthouses which still operate today.

The single shop and pub on Lundy is the Marisco Tavern & General Store. Named after one-time owners of the island, the pub was famous for having no licensing hours, although whether it stayed open or not was up to the landlord.

The steep path up from the landing beach.

The severe-looking St Helena's Church on Lundy was built by one-time owner Revd H.G. Heaven in 1897. It was equipped with a peal of eight bells and apparently 'many cottages were demolished' during its construction.

This rather sad-looking boat is the *mv Lerina*, a 72-ton Lowestoft drifter that acted as the main link between Lundy and Bideford for many years. When Martin Harman purchased the island in 1925 for £16,000 he inherited the boat and its captain, Fred Dark, as well. A common sight in North Devon, it loaded and unloaded at Instow and Bideford and was in constant service until November 1950 (apart from the war years when it was commandeered by the Navy). This photograph was taken in June 1953 and shows the vessel beached at Cleave, Northam. Eventually it was sold as scrap for just £1 – a sad end to its very chequered history, which included being a mail packet, a passenger (and farm animal) ferry, a PoW transporter and a RN auxiliary patrol vessel, which was used in secret experiments to lay an oil pipeline from Britain to France following D-Day.

The word 'romantic' is often used in connection with the island of Lundy – so what better place to get married? In February 1952 the 75-year-old vicar of Appledore, Revd H. Muller, took his first ever flight to fly from Chivenor to Lundy to officiate at the wedding of John Robinson and Jean Crabtree in St Helena's Church on the island. Jean was a niece of F.W. Gade, the island's agent, and had acted as Lundy's postmistress on occasions. The congregation numbered just 19 and included off-duty light-housemen and farm workers – all

of whom later crowded into the Marisco Tavern for the reception. This was only the fifth ever wedding on Lundy and the first since 1938.

CHAPTER NINE
THE LYNMOUTH FLOOD DISASTER

On Friday, 15 August 1952 the East and West Lyn rivers, enormously swollen by weeks of heavy rain, overwhelmed the village of Lynmouth and killed 34 people. The devastation was enormous and both the Army and the other public services were engaged for months afterwards in the cleaning-up and rebuilding operations. The damage caused is apparent from this series of shots.

One of the first man-made features to be destroyed was Barbrook Bridge, high up the West Lyn. During the fatal flood an Army DUKW attempted to cross the river but found it impossible. Here we see a temporary bridge being put in place.

On the East Lyn, Hillsford Bridge was destroyed and here again the Army stepped in and erected a temporary Bailey bridge to restore communications and ensure the reconstruction operation went smoothly.

Most of the destruction of the Lynmouth flood disaster was concentrated in the centre of the village and the awesome power of moving water is shown clearly in these dramatic photographs.

Lynmouth wasn't the only settlement to be affected by the rivers pouring off Exmoor. Parracombe, set in the moor's foothills, was also devastated as this photograph clearly shows.

Within weeks local businesses were up and running again as best they could. Here, the village tobacconist William Nicholls is seen with his wife serving the officer in charge of Army operations and Chief Fire Officer Hart. At the time when this was taken in the first week of September 1952, Mr Nicholls was reported as saying 'Business is fair'.

The following month Prince Philip, accompanied by the Lord Lieutenant of Devon, Earl Fortescue, visited Lynmouth to express solidarity with the local people, who, even though their world had been turned upside down, managed to put on a hearty welcome.

Residents who had been made homeless in the disaster were temporarily rehoused in caravans at nearby Holman Park. Six of these had been given by people shocked at the disaster who wanted to help the survivors in some practical way. The camp was open from August 1952 until March 1953.

On the first anniversary of the disaster the Chairman of Lynton and Lynmouth Council, Tom Bevan, accompanied by his councillors, laid a wreath on the communal grave of some of the victims in the local cemetery.

CHAPTER TEN
SCHOOLS AND YOUNG PEOPLE

Following the Second World War there was a massive 'baby boom' and by the 1950s new schools had to be built to cope with all the young children. In July 1954 the Forches Primary School was opened in Barnstaple by G.C. Hayter Hames, Vice-Chairman of Devon County Council. In his speech he reckoned that 'An age could be judged by the provision it made for the education of its children.' These are noble sentiments when one considers that this one school cost £35,942, a huge sum at that date.

After the war there was an enormous 'rationalisation' of village schools with many small ones being closed. Amongst them was Chaloner's School in Braunton, which was named after Revd William Chaloner who in 1667 left a legacy of £450 to establish the foundation. Originally based in a room next to the local church-yard it moved to its Georgeham Cross site in 1854. In July 1949 the Governors announced that it was to close forthwith and these photographs were taken as a record of a well-loved school, through whose doors generations of North Devonians had passed.

The post-war baby boom was accompanied by a massive increase in State help to both mothers and their offspring. This was delivered via a series of welfare clinics held in villages and towns throughout the country. This photograph, from January 1950, shows mothers and babies attending the Fremington clinic, held in the parish hall under the direction of Miss Edwards, the local health visitor.

In 1942 a day nursery was opened in Oakleigh Road, Barnstaple to care for the children of women engaged in war work. It was so successful that an announcement that it was to be closed in 1949 brought a storm of protest from both mothers and the local Chamber of Commerce, 'who feared that the result would be a depletion of the labour force so necessary for the export drive'. Always over-subscribed, this view shows some of the 40 who attended, playing on their climbing-frame.

A group of pupils play hopscotch in the playground of the Bideford Church Infants School in 1954. The school was built on the corner of High and Honestone Streets on land given by the Bideford Bridge Trust in 1845. It was designed to hold 120 pupils and was always crowded. Today's pupils go to St Mary's School and the old building now houses the Bideford Angling Club.

Maypole dancers in Pilton in August 1949. The original caption noted, 'As in all young performers grace and courtliness comes quite naturally to them.'

A crowd of interested Bideford school pupils crowd around the gangplank of the *Lundy Gannet* to watch 30 sheep being taken out to the island in October 1956. The movement back and forth of animals (and tourists) still draws a crowd today.

In the period before the 'school run' became a seemingly permanent feature of parents' days, most schoolchildren either walked or cycled. The police operated an inspection regime for cycles and here we see PCs Howick and Addicott checking machines owned by boys of the Braunton Secondary Modern School in November 1956.

High Bickington is a village with a strong sense of community and in 1953 it could boast enough Scouts, Guides, Cubs and Brownies to stage a 'special dedication service' on St George's Day.

I have used a fair few pictures of Scouts and Guides in this book if only because they were very popular youth organisations in the 1950s. This particular view shows a happy crowd of Guides from the Sticklepath area of Barnstaple off to their annual camp at Croyde in July 1952.

Barnstaple Square is shown here in April 1956 when some 500 Scouts, Girl Guides, Cubs and Brownies from all over North Devon took part in the largest St George's Day parade since the war. The Bideford Church Lads' Brigade Band provided the music and District Commissioner H.J. Tyreman took the salute as the procession made its way to Trinity Church.

The school curriculum today always seems to be in a state of flux with subjects being added or subtracted on a fairly constant basis. No local school, however, now gives lessons in falconry as Braunton Secondary Modern did in July 1950! Here we see Michael Berry and Trevor Osborne admiring Kiki, one of the school's kestrel hawks. Apparently Kiki had flown away twice but 'so good is the treatment she receives from the boys that she has returned to the hawkhouse each time.'

Perhaps equally unexpected today is this picture of children learning how to make cheese at Barnstaple Secondary Modern School, as they did in April 1954.

Domestic Science lessons were clearly fun if this photograph of the girls of the Barnstaple Secondary Modern School, who had produced some 150 Christmas cakes between November and December 1956, is anything to go by.

School life was not all classroom based of course and here we see students at Chulmleigh Secondary Modern School taking part in a 'Chariot' race at their Sports Day in 1952.

These boys from Braunton Secondary Modern school were also outside a classroom, but in this case they were learning various farming skills, including stonewalling as shown here in July 1950.

In September 1952 the newly-built North Devon Technical College opened on its site at the top of Sticklepath Hill and the occasion was recorded in these two photographs, showing boys being instructed in the then very modern engineering shops. The college later dropped the 'Technical' from its title and now provides a vast range of practical and academic subjects.

Childrens' crazes are commonplace today but in post-war Britain the first major one was the Davy Crockett hat. A Saturday-morning cinema serial, a film and appearances in comics saw the furry hat with 'coonskin' tail attached become a common feature of most boys' wardrobes. A query by a *Journal-Herald* reporter in February 1956, wondering who would be the first to wear the hat in North Devon, resulted in this photograph of 13-year-old Wilfred Ashelford of Umberleigh, who had been lucky enough to be sent one (plus a lumberman's jacket and a Bowie knife) from a relative in Ontario, Canada 'where the fashion is all the rage among the youngsters now.'

Looking excited, a crowd of children from Instow School are seen on a school trip to Fremington in June 1955. They may not have gone very far but clearly they were pleased to get out of their classrooms.

The Bideford Regatta has been held for at least 150 years and is one of the high points of the North Devon sporting calendar. In 1951 the event was held in drizzling rain but still drew crowds four to five deep along the entire quayside. They saw only one local victory when the Bideford Ladies Rowing Club 'A'

team won the Bruford Challenge Cup. During the day a coal vessel, the *David M*, arrived and was soon berthed – only to be 'invaded by spectators grateful for this unexpected grandstand'. One innovation was the use of walkie-talkie radio sets by marshals to help control the day's events. The Chairman of the organising committee was G. Blackman and the two Regatta Secretaries were Jack Fulford and Arthur Pearson.

CHAPTER ELEVEN
❧ SPORTS ❧

One of the local events that still sporadically occurs is the pancake race. Combe Martin was noted for its long run of these, one of which is captured in this photograph, which shows the contest in 1954. The winner was No.8, Mrs E. Hartley, with the runners-up being Mrs B. Edwards and Mrs G. M. Tossell.

This rather bizarre photograph from October 1951 records a 'swimming machine', constructed by C.J. Webber who appears on the right. He had constructed it for members of the Barnstaple Swimming Club who, we are told, 'will derive much benefit from its use during the winter.'

This fine action shot captures A. Morley of Wrafton taking a steep bank on his Ariel motorcycle at the North Devon Motor Club's 'Novices' and Observers' trials held at Hartnoll Barton, Muddiford in March 1952.

In March 1954 the Devon County Amateur Athletics Association held the Ross Shield Road Race through the streets of Barnstaple for the first time. The winning team came from Paignton, whilst the individual winner was P. Perry of the Exeter Harriers – he is wearing the dark vest in the photograph and his victory was said to be 'an easy win'.

Owing to the steepness and seeming ubiquity of hills in North Devon cycling has never been as popular as elsewhere, but here we see local enthusiasts in Barnstaple at the start of the 50-mile Taw Valley cycle race one Sunday morning in June 1953. It was taken near where the present-day fire station stands.

A 'splash night' from May 1954 at the old Ilfracombe swimming pool, held to inaugurate a new season of the local swimming club. The pool was originally constructed for the use of guests staying at the Ilfracombe Hotel which itself was opened in 1867. It later became the town's Municipal Baths.

In August 1952 the North Devon Motor Club staged a grass-track meeting at Fremington for those members who drove motorcycles. The picture shows P. Heard of Bideford on a 350 Enfield leading the field in the race for bikes of unlimited engine size. Unfortunately he was later overtaken and finished third. Before the meeting the vicar of Fremington denounced the Sunday event saying that it 'attacks Christian worship'.

In 1950 Walter Bond, a Barnstaple accountant, resurrected the old Barnstaple and North Devon Flying Club. Based at Chivenor it provided the mail service to Lundy as well as offering training and pleasure flights. Here we see Miss Sheelagh Glover, a nurse at North Middlesex Hospital, and Walter Bond (left) after receiving a flying lesson from Maurice Looker (right) in May 1952.

People still look slightly askance at female footballers but in North Devon they extend back to at least the first decades of the twentieth century. Here, from May 1951, are Kathleen Darch and Margaret Taylor, captains of the Combe Martin and Woolacombe womens' soccer teams, shaking hands before a match which Combe Martin went on to win. The man is referee Arthur Pearce. The two teams appear below.

CHAPTER TWELVE

❧ A MISCELLANY ❧

These three striking photographs show Chanter's Folly, which used to stand above the large quarry now used by Appledore shipyard. Built in 1819 by local merchant Thomas Chanter, it was, the story goes, used by him to watch for his returning vessels in order to expedite their unloading. Hit by lightning in 1927 and badly damaged by fire in 1945 it eventually became so unsafe that it had to be demolished by the local Council in late 1952.

Then, as now, politicians often appeared in the pages of local newspapers and when an election was held in October 1951 three candidates put their names forward. Here we see the Conservative Brigadier, C. Peto, canvassing in a Barnstaple coal yard. He went on to win with 19,780 votes, being followed by W. Wilkey for Labour with 10,632 and Alse Halse for the Liberals with 7,326.

The first ever picture of Jeremy Thorpe to appear in the *Journal-Herald* came in July 1952. The ever-dapper politician was just 23 years old and as President of the Oxford Union had journeyed to Barnstaple to talk to local Liberals. Prophetically it was noted that 'Mr Thorpe said he would pay further visits to the constituency.'

Anyone looking at a map of North Devon can only be impressed by the wide mouth of the Taw and Torridge estuaries. Unfortunately a shifting sandbank makes entrance for ships dangerous and in 1820 a lighthouse was erected at Crow Point on Braunton Burrows. Known as the Bideford High Light it was a manned facility until 1950 when the buildings were deemed unsuitable for the keepers. Economic conditions precluded provision of a new lighthouse and eventually the structure was demolished, with an automatic beacon erected at Instow to guide ships in.

This remarkable car was the work of P. Pooley of Newport in Barnstaple who built it in his father's cycle workshop over three years to solve the problem of the long waiting lists for new cars after the war. Powered by a 350cc motorcycle engine the two-seater could cruise at 35mph and after its inaugural trip in February 1949 it became a common sight in the area.

With the spread of cars came motoring competitions. One type was the 'one gallon rally', where cars had to travel over a set distance on a measured amount of fuel. Here we see one such event starting off from Elliott's Garage in Bideford in February 1957. The 20-mile rally was won by Norman Weeks with his navigator Jack Jones.

Even though 1950s cars travelled far slower than today they still managed to be crashed with some regularity, often with fatal results. In June 1950 an 18-year-old soldier from Fremington Camp was killed at Instow Cross when his car crashed into a Bideford-based lorry. His two companions were seriously injured.

This horrific crash occurred in May 1949 at Langridgeford when Frank McBride from Dumfries crashed his cattle lorry. The roof of the vehicle was chopped open with axes to release the ten uninjured pedigree Ayrshire cattle he was carrying.

With the growth of private-car ownership before the war, pedestrians began to become 'second-class' road users and to help redress the balance the Government, under its transport minister Leslie Hore-Belisha, introduced the 'zebra' crossing. The first one in North Devon was constructed in Ilfracombe and here we see it on its opening day in July 1953 – complete with its 'belisha' beacons.

This dramatic derailing occurred in May 1959 when a petrol tanker holding 4,000 gallons of fuel overturned in the Barnstaple Victoria Road Station good's yard. Local firemen stood by for six hours as petrol seeped out and was caught in cans by employees of the oil company. The tanker was eventually lifted back on the rails by a mobile crane especially brought from Exeter.

In today's world, where 18-year-old students regularly set off on 'gap' years to travel the world, no newspaper editor would bother publishing a photograph like the one above. In May 1955, however, the idea that four Barnstaple nurses could go on a motorcycling holiday to Paris and Italy made the front page. They don't seem to have much luggage with them though!

This lovely vessel was the ketch, *Enid,* moored at Vellator, Braunton in August 1951. She was being prepared for a round-the-world voyage by her owners, 32-year-old C.P.B. Stevenson and his wife Eileen, with the help of Captain E.G. Coates, a retired ship's master of South Street in Braunton. The ship had been built at Milford Haven in 1900 and cost the Stevensons £1,500.

Every village in North Devon at one time had one or more 'clubs'. These were Friendly Societies whose members paid a weekly contribution and, during times of illness, received benefit payments. Many also ensured members were given a decent burial, thus escaping the stigma of a pauper's funeral. One important aspect of the club was its annual meeting and meal, often accompanied by a procession through the village. Most had disappeared with the introduction of the National Insurance scheme but a few survived and here we see the Chawleigh Club Walk in June 1952.

The Lynton Cliff Railway, seen here in 1949, was designed by local man Bob Jones and financed by Sir George Newnes, a prominent Victorian publisher. It was opened on 9 April 1890 by Lady Jeune, the lady of the manor. Based on a hydraulic lift system it used 700 gallons of water ballast in each 'car' to help raise passengers through a vertical height of some 500 feet.

Just to show that nothing is new I have included this shot of Barnstaple Square in July 1956, where local OAPs are seen protesting about the low level of their pensions. The marchers had sent a petition to the Prime Minister and one of them was reported as saying 'What are the old people going to do this winter, if the price of coal remains the same as it is today?'

Televisions were uncommon in the 1950s so one can imagine how pleased the young inmates of the Barnstaple Cottage Homes (built as the juvenile section of the Workhouse) were, being given one in February 1955. The donors were the members of the Social Club at Messrs Ayers and Grimshaw and the photograph shows the Matron, Mrs A. Hicks, and some of her charges with the works Foreman, C. Knapman, the Secretary, A. Clements, and W. Screech, the Treasurer of the club.

In April 1956 the *Journal-Herald* reported the discovery of a 'What-is-it animal' about 'the size of a rat, with dark brown fur, long hind legs, and features almost similar to a young dog.' It was discovered by Mr I. Warren of South Molton, who was out ferreting when his ferret was badly mauled after being sent down a rabbit hole. Its attacker followed the injured ferret out, whereupon Warren shot it. He thought it was a cross between a dog and a fox but after consulting the Natural History Museum in London he learnt it was merely a fox cub - although it was noted that it was 'unusual for fox cubs to be seen out of their burrows at such an early age.'

In August 1929 Henry Williamson, the author of *Tarka the Otter*, then newly arrived in the area, was caught after defacing the Georgeham village sign. In a strange echo of that event some 26 years later this signpost at Heanton was rearranged to read 'No halt in hell' and 'A thin hole'. One could be forgiven for wondering if Williamson was the culprit.

The photograph on the left shows the oddest thing in this book – a 'tramps' town', discovered in a coppice at Fremington in January 1946. A local tramp, George Stuart, died aged 61 and at his inquest the police were asked to investigate where he lived. When they found the site they discovered a motley collection of shacks built out of US Army surplus material and scrap metal. There was even a canvas kennel complete with a straw mattress. The police proceeded to burn the huts down to zencourage the tramps to move on.

A Clovelly wedding between Royston Johns and Jill Olney in September 1956. As they processed down the steep cobbled main street 'Visitors bowed to the bride, and fishermen and their families threw confetti and wished her luck.' Royston is now the Torridge District Councillor for Clovelly.

North Devon has experienced some hard winters but in February 1947 the weather turned so cold, with some 13 degrees of frost, that the River Taw froze at Barnstaple. Milkmen found their churns frozen solid, schools were closed and Barnstaple's Friday Pannier Market had only three stalls present. Two doctors trying to reach a pregnant Challacombe woman could only get to her using skis and horses.

Compare the youthful members of today's Croyde Surf Lifesaving Club with those belonging to the Croyde Life Saving Unit, here pictured in August 1950. They were photographed whilst practising for the annual Negley Farson trophy, competed for by teams from the coastal areas between Watchet and Hartland. Mr Farson gave the trophy after his son Daniel was saved by the Clovelly lifeboat when in imminent danger of drowning at Baggy Point.

The rocket apparatus carried a rope to ships in danger and allowed a breeches buoy to be set up. It might look primitive but it helped save many lives.

In December 1956 South Molton Amateur Football Club distributed ten tons of logs to local OAPs. Here, the Club Secretary, Albert Whitefield, and the Chair of the Women's Committee, Mrs P. Shapland, presents one hundredweight of wood to 90-year-old John Metters.

In 1605 John Andrew, a rich merchant and fishing-boat owner, willed that the annual rent from a field he owned in Bideford be spent to supply bread to the poor of the town. Here, in January 1956, we see the Deputy Mayor, C. Cann, assisted by the Mayor's Secretary, Miss J. Bedingfield, carrying out John's wishes. The land is now the playing field of Bideford College and the rent is still distributed annually, though now it is in the form of money payments. The trustees still hold an annual meal where, under the terms of their founder's will, they eat salt cod – to commemorate the source of Andrew's wealth.

This view, taken at Appledore in October 1952, shows the *Kathleen and May*. Built and named the *Lizzie May* at Connah's Quay on the Dee estuary in North Wales at a cost of £2,700, she was employed for many years in the general coasting trade, carrying cargoes such as coal, bricks and fertilisers. Sold in 1908 to Martin Fleming of Youghal in Eire, she was renamed the *Kathleen and May* and then resold in 1931 to William Jewell of Appledore who fitted her with a diesel engine. She was taken out of service in 1960, eventually being brought back to North Devon and is currently moored alongside Bideford Bridge whilst her future is decided.

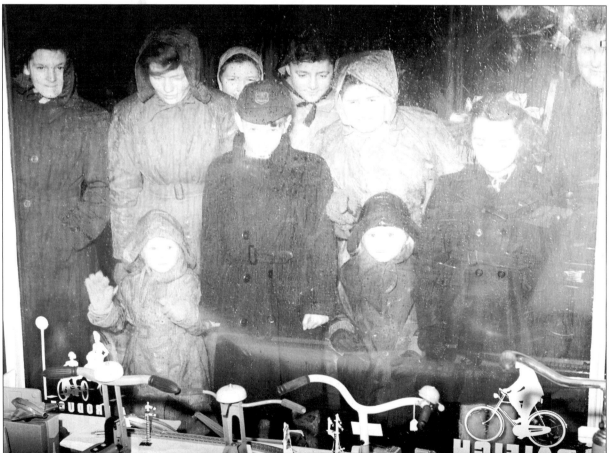

This last picture is one of my favourites. In the post-war years austerity was still a way of life and spending money was hard to come by. I well recall being taken on my father's bike to 'window shop' before Christmas, when I could look all I wanted knowing full well that I couldn't have everything I desired, yet getting huge pleasure from just looking. Here, from Christmas 1952, we see a crowd of window shoppers in Barnstaple looking longingly at a display of bicycles and scooters.

INDEX